Personification

Personification

poems by Margaret Ronda

winner of the Saturnalia Books Poetry Prize
selected by Carl Phillips

saturnalia books

Saturnalia Books
105 Woodside Rd.
Ardmore, PA 19003
info@saturnaliabooks.com

ISBN: 978-0-9818591-5-6
Library of Congress Control Number: 2009933614

Book Design by Saturnalia Books
Printing by Westcan Printing Group, Canada

Cover Art: Joachim Patinir, "Landscape with St. Jerome."
Courtesy of the Museo del Prado, Madrid.

Author photo credit: Tobias Menely

Distributed by:
University Press of New England
1 Court Street
Lebanon, NH 03766
800-421-1561

Thanks to the editors of the journals and anthologies where these poems appeared, sometimes in different form: *AGNI*, *Argotist*, *Berkeley Poetry Review*, *Best New Poets 2007*, *Eleventh Muse*, *Fourteen Hills*, *Ghosting Atoms: Notes and Reflections After the Bomb*, *Gulf Coast*, *Pool*, *Portland Review*, *Salamander*, *Seattle Review*, *Xantippe*.

Abiding gratitude for your inspiration and wisdom to Charlie Altieri, Julie Carr, Linda Carroll, Jessica Fisher, Hillary Gravendyk, Robert Hass, Lyn Hejinian, Brenda Hillman, Michelle Ross, Brian Teare, and Elizabeth Marie Young. Thanks to Henry Israeli and Carl Phillips for supporting this project.

Special thanks to my father, Bruce Ronda, and to my late mother, Priscilla Inkpen, whose graceful and generous spirit continues to guide me every day.

Table of Contents

for Tobias

For allegory, far from truly being a "personification," instead expresses precisely the impossibility of the person.

—Giorgio Agamben

Postcard

Travelled inside the sea wall, gauzy net, hole
in summer's dress, losing color with each
breath, the seashore inward in the mornings.
Some early days stricken, possibly with rain,
and we forgot how to entirely. A sea held
under its surface, redrawn, and so what we
composed was less than ideal. Yet still
we hurried, if only to find ourselves folded
inside the same palest chance. It was a story
we told countlessly, each time revising
the end. The hills disappeared into the sea.
But nothing passed through the seismic
blockade, even the waves were simply rumors.
We thought of it as a frame, and inside,
thickened time, something we could almost
hold. Like water, but sadder, disloyal.

Recitative

Small bird split open inside your chest. A dream and then drift.
Someone opened the wrong door. You could remember the red
blouse and nothing else. As if folded into a crease. We set off
toward the four corners, holding down the sky.

And above you were an iron bird. Warm, still breathing in my
hands. I worried about your irregular heart. You're one of a kind,
someone said. Six buttons, pearly slick, lined on the tongue. I
could never catch the answer.

Then we were climbing into a cloud, or the stuck light inside a
bottle. The dream is following me, you kept saying. Finger along a
white stitch. Trudging up red hills, though the sky called us back.
I'd stopped listening to the plastic bird's song.

Our time is up, someone said. You had cut the top off each picture.
Later I found the box of skies. Red and unfastening. O but we
dreamed to mend. Only the glass bird I called Question, crack in
the forehead where the wind comes through.

Sonnet

And we lived inside it. It mingled in cloudless supplications,
something unbreathable. Our hands funneling, twine untwine in
narrow rows. Painted green as languish, copper as the sea. Inside
were golden things, phosphorus of camera flash or field burning,
we laid under filaments: iron and satellite. Blurred, as in not yet,
not new, only aftermath of white paper we had written our names
on. We lived in winter, where it turned twelve colors before our
eyes. Or grew heavier, more secretive, alive in its pearly shell.
Nothing inside the rooms we left alone, no coal burnt to cinders.
Back to decimals hushed and furious, not to skip the blueprint of
sky scratched with care on the eyelid. Back to amoretti shiny as
rust. The barest disturbance echoed in wall-sized waves. Just a
fraction, specimen of wild design. Something faltering, we wanted
to say miraculous, run our fingers along the intricate bracework,
but how airless it was.

The New World

already awake and bleating. Orange crush stain round its mouth but I
am not ready to marry you. What compact cinched me sheet-white in
folds of sleep. A feeble siren, cold air chokes, the address had my name
on it. Sewn in rectangles of freeway light, or was it the radio excited by
war. Durable veils start by uncreating, toss a gauzy film between me
and praise. A formal mist. Early December static slits the voice into
angry and broken. That every man strives to accommodate himself to
the rest is a law no man can shirk.

So the creek's gone down again, but the fog is thick. Wakefulness is a
gold band around the neck. What abides without reflection, dream's
muck, a few indigestable phrases, a coat with an orange in the pocket.

Rough to the touch, untranslatable, not a natural fact. Only the fabric
remained, heavy on the shoulders. Some mornings you just want to
laugh and be done with it, but that means you've lost your focus. Or
face. Every day begins in weather and ends in nightly news. In
between, a series of parcels and servers.

Amid the infinite graces of the solicitous, a certain cold-eyed scrutiny.
To avoid this I rarely make eye contact. But all the talk's of diplomacy,
the silkiness of men in gray suits. The morning is headed toward snow,
stopping short. Each figure's features unmarked, even the sun shrugs off
an approach. No one here I know, and there may be a pleasure in this,
mixed with spite.

No-no of the day: civil war. So shrapnel and improvised devices devise new impolitics. Here civil's courtesy needs hostility, a law needs its exception, the air needs the cars to pummel it furiously. If I was crying in the coffeeshop, it was for the man who shredded his map along the path, so as to be found.

The day breeds habits, like the woman bundling her hands. Dog paws to go out, whines, I make something boil, another for the trash, I brush the carpet, dry the furnace, apply a berry stain, I flinch at the mail, color my skin, weave a hand-size knot to crawl inside. And we're off to the park.

But I was talking about the light, how unwilled it feels. Involuntary as being stuck in a damaged hour, not knowing enough to wake. Self-government is the goal, but is perhaps unachievable. If a face stops circulating, diminishing value sets in, that is the law of the market. An orange leaf skimming the creek casts no shadow I can see.

The validity of covenants: or, how many ways to file the claim. First, understand what your policies cover. Second, keep records of all your expenses. Third, protect your assets in case of fire, flood, earthquake, hurricane, theft, accident, or other loss. If you fail to follow these simple rules, you may be subject to forfeiture or devaluation. And when a covenant is made, to break it is unjust, and whatsoever is not unjust, is just.

Oh hush, said the room, but the cellphone kept chirruping. *Pursue*:
to harass, worry, torment, or to prosecute, follow in order, chase,
undertake an endeavor, or to proceed with no end in sight. Forever
pressing in, the uninvited guest at the screen door.

Today I made myself accountable to currency's flows, shifted my body
around in the stream.

A voice speaking to me only, even if it's mine, has a certain pitch.
Speech isn't just thought out loud. Should I answer it? Steadily
I listened, but each note slid away, missing its cause, already up the
stairs and asleep in another room. As if to say, dreamer, disturb not my
sound slumber. I followed the thought a long time, waking everyone
with my footfall.

Sympathy

After a while we went through a sheet of humidity, said something that was almost the truth. Not a curtain, the yellow shone along it, slightly bent. But we were inattentive guests, holding our breath while what gleamed in the apartment. So it seemed overcast, discounting the tense strip of heat stretching between us. The white walls made a screen we pushed against gently.

We spoke or didn't. Each murmur a corridor to disappear into. A syntax we missed, and so the room was divided into an awning and shade, the sun ignoring us completely. A list of things not to say, hoarded up. Around us, everyone we loved passing by. Still that feeling like someone is staring at you, a white line down the back.

Inside that black square where you go before words find you. Impossibly whole, for just a moment, and together there. Then our skin transparent again. And all fog, a muffled room where something keeps rolling in.

In The Arcades

We stepped through the weather
toward that mill of instruction: the reading room
where strangers shuffled in double-time
kicking up asterisks of dust

cloaked in their velveteen remove
paintings spared us a moral
but each book foretold our journey as arduous
rehearsing a glove-like logic, in which nothing
happens to history

how pinned we were, how nowhere
thus we feasted on the snowy index
where all lies marvelously came true

a thoughtful person opened a window
so the embroidered animals could get some air
white heron with its yellow sunspots
hovered above twenty eyeless bulls

the lights flickering off made the room sultry & plush
we dropped heavier into the crumbling pages
our eyelids grew languid, profitless
as outside the glassworks burned

Aria

Shine without contour,
absence becoming
the scene, a kind
of unrecognition

or impatience.
As in a dream, where
the unlocatable
bird expands in song,

enfolds the street
you follow down,
no searching will
uncloister its red

noise in your chest,
throat-flutter where
the stitch of the
hem came loose,

that face you can't
find. You are
climbing inside
a ripped-up night,

the light wrung
out. The bird has no
wings: it can't be
measured by the eye.

Bad Architecture

News of a bombing meant none of us were transparent.
Our hands touched backwards. Then we watched morning
come in spatters, tea down a shirt. We put our feet one by one
into it, blue with spots of pink in the center. Trains came and went
carrying their secrets. We found ourselves urged. Taking the form
of tamped-down snow on a field. When the light made its way
toward us, we wondered where we could stand: so much
gashed out, or blue with furious burns. Here or here. Nowhere
to arrive at, just white-ash buildings with holes for eyes.
Something, shadows maybe, moving around inside.

Bovary

watching for someone else
      o   my clean couch

rumbling garbage truck hailstorm bag of
mustard greens
               nouns postman or the Arts
& squirrels up yesterday's tree

impossible husbandry
      of gaudy
spring in the provinces

       the will flutters in every wind
string of
      bad whims or dust-trail
         still clothed

another vexed conversation
               sans context
eyes lowered in
      garish anticipation
         each desire   has its budget
but what great task
      to recline
           too long
      under rainy gusts of
the unremarkable

warm as a captive dove

someone
      force the window forge
               the form
          cash the check or just
    lie here

Short Fiction

Watch the sky, was the key phrase. So I have been. It's gotten darker around the edges. At the page's center, a bruise of rain. And the air so stumble-drunk with heat, bullying. Someone keeps leaving messages, a voice I don't know. I'll just keep trying, it says. Everything green is scalded. Crumpled and sour. Swimmers at the lake scatter at the sound of thunder. The rain like iron, then the sun shuts it all down. In the page the words are emblems etched along the shoreline. To withdraw from the world to wait and in waiting find. All day the water destroys them.

Captivity Narrative

So far had we walked, through such faintness and forsaken ground,
that we were unprepared:

the whole village being on fire and the flames exactly symmetrical,
the grasses on fire and the people darkly running in a row,

smoke in the throat of it,
the hour burning now in the shape of a cross.

And all around, a bristling in the trees, a circling, a swallow-call:
as if raised above and reeling.

For it is said of incidental signs:

That a fire in one's path is an indication of misfortune, as is
wandering in a swamp, and the sight of red flowers,

and the flames rising to the left, then separating into many parts,
changing from snow to a fierce orange.

Mouths full of dirt, we could barely hear the order. A distance off,
laughing or screaming.

Meanwhile the houses blackened to zero. Meanwhile the veil.

North and south, a loosing of wind, the fire lamenting our skirts.

Softly, cinder.
Softly, burr of smoke clouding the way:

the whole prairie now, all its westward grasses—

Black Square

It was west and then sleep, a blue screen we could not
walk through. String of goldfish in unlit rooms, a capsulated
dream of strict eavesdropping. Half listening, wandering
into bony havens of birdsong. Then recalled by a little
scar in conversation. A kind of light stopped in the orange gill.
At last lulled from kindness by the darker square, a condensed
unparticular numbness. A minus sign glows the murky water.

Short Fiction

Feeling bored, I flung myself down in the page. Everything seemed
normal: the green grass, a flag fluttering, some talk of a trip.
Looking more closely, I saw it was a description of how the mind
works: first the sense, then its symptom. The flag became an arrow
pointing me toward the oldest story, of a pilgrim's journey
chastened by ruin. The home was burnt with bales of flax and
hemp, the children were stolen away, and the tone grew allegorical.
Meanwhile, the sun had burnt a hole in the grass. Hot on the side
of the face. The heat was in my head, the way I thought about it. It
wasn't that the sun had returned, just that I looked up.

Fateful Tale

A wood of half-intent
               watery incidents shot in foxlight

            & you my faithful companion
                     sent your color ahead as scout

        all is october in these woods

            surely the red-gowned trees stood
                for a spot of time drawing closed

how cloudy we had become with fate

        bedded down in the dense understory
           we lay amidst mosses
                leaves lidded with wren and mercury

    their sweet *ee-oh-layyy* clothed our slumber

    undreaming lulled us pathless
                    even our inward eye slept

thickly the lake water rose
              soaking yellow

the late hyssop

inciting errant weeds
　　　to a fast enclosure about us

　　　　　　　green we slept darker and hushed
til a grove-bird's piercing cry bestirred

o we have fallen forgetful out of season
　　　　　　　　this too the illusion of freedom

now must we walk without the sun

Envoy

yellow lightband
took off its face
eyeholes
scrubbed out pieces
poured and poured out

*

cover each caught
place, cautious stare
downslope
come out come out
but liar day

*

nobody dust
broken persuade
chalk-mouth
grainy strict no
ladder unclimb

meadow a boast
faith wears gray boots
stamping
undertruth cut
or in the ear

*

pale pressing wince
flung mistrust wide
outsize
astringent throat
overhearing

*

silicate ebb
verge of bright split
certain
concord of glass
unbreak, untie

a rack of clouds
slant in the blue
unshore
persuaded face
it is not you

*

hammering in
storm-privacy
small coin
flung in fever
said go away

*

forsake proceed
yellow light-hole
where are
dropped and sinking
eyelid under

*

pieces not the whole
flower not the whole
little wound
or a slip down
foxglove wasps nest
sting on the finger
abyss: a bit of ego

Character Study

Was it a mirror I was looking for? Better go get dressed and take a look. A wine-stained mouth is like a day-lily, paint on a fender, or the crumpled wrapper in the trash, depending. My expression cloudy, stormy, civil, composed. But if no simile runs on all four legs, how partial am I, walking down the stairs in ill-fitting clothes.

Prodigal desire to be outside in other air or yesterday's wayside. Bound by sliding words, sleeping with an eye color, penning an impossible letter. If I had changed the shape of my shirt—but it's no use, the description holds. One more way to be found, or waylaid by sound. Today's walls bend morning to their will, a reflection is handmaiden to its face. In this way I am both empty and full.

Persons and Things

End of the month, rice and beer, no wine.
Landlocked on State Street, rain crowds
smart-bound paper-ready customers of the insider
experience. Shape-shifters demand a dollar-fifty,
the astral and Shelleyan lights.

I am an eye-level sign that dances on the corner,
A made-up flophouse with no vacancy.
You are wheels and feet, a neighbor shifting
his weight behind the makeshift partition.

Now is the consumer's time, unsold goods stacking up
and IOU cards they boil into a kind of soup.
A leather chair, a marked-down silk-linen sweater, a line
of surplus credit you may be, the woman hangs onto
the phone inside her head and lets her voice drop.

I am the guardian of many persons, in the shape of
a church, jewel, or a fountain. I am wearing my skin.
You are not a visionary; you would like a cold
soda or a can of fresh pussy, please.

Fair enough, the store motto, but toxic assets
confront shareholders in shabby disguises.
Repeating the word *shutter* makes the mouth
sore. The man ran into the margin and curled up
in the deficit, the girl grew organic eggs.

Walking Late

Then up ahead, the man with the blue shirt. Follow me he said.
The pink camellias glared flat-eyed.

Car after car passing, tinny red taillights. How many bones
in the body. A line drawn through it.

Circuitry of paths, one meant to lie. Then we were abandoned
by lawns, and concrete sprang up in meadows.

He said stay close. I could smell his skin. Ribcage pushed
against the hand.

Hastening now, and sometimes a boy running out a back door.
Or a cloud pulling apart above us.

I left a trail of silver rings hanging on branches. A nest threaded,
a maze. And how to say hold back, hold.

I see the hills he said. They've split you open. Night by
now, kids setting off fireworks down the street.

Half-circles of sparks, then black.

Called Away

As if a tiny tear in fabric. A burst blood vessel. And inside, so many
wavering threads, silk to the touch, going nowhere. The air stayed sealed.
It was orange, aggressive. A sound like velvet stingers brushing past.

Above, people shuffling on, motiveless. Someone was cursing, dragging
a sweater in the dirt. Elbows pinned to my waist. Perhaps a rash across
my eyes.

Gurgling in the chest. A warble, a bit of rust in the lungs, dimly felt.
White flecks in the air like shredded kleenex. Twenty names dotting
my throat. But never burned straight clear. I could say shivering but
the skin is such a comfort.

How many days of always noon. Someone never calling my name. Just
the needle's eye, and I threaded over and over.

Always an End

Moth tapping and the voice: *slow down*. A night-place, trying to
hold still. But the red numbers husking.

The passage so narrow, dark bruises on legs. Whatever else
was rain down a gutter.

In the dream, the car burned itself out. Lying down in the soot
and charred metal. Bits of glass. How they turn suddenly to snow,
and cold splinters the back.

Red numbers saying *here, here*.

Caught reaching backward. Feeling for a length of white
cloth, sound of gravel. A netting thrown over the body, crawling.
Was it the air, pressing in? A knee on the chest?

So hard to remember. A punched-out hour. Something faintly
breathing, underneath.

Phosphoric

eyes ears caked with fire sand erupts in hair as ash as bone as saliva
so we rattled teeth on triggers stuffed pockets with tokens of a
lesser sun a fiery blister we drank clouded face lashed face the
flagged black wore horizon's mask headlights public eyes a white
flare a hum under breath calcified in air moved nowhere but white
assembled us as dust as scoured earth nowhere we were not tire
marks a door blown off its hinge and still writhing phosphoric
with improvised light a thought without homeland soaked in ruin
and ordinary time

The Storm in Fancy's Meadow

and I a ward a jacob's bed long and weary road
so trod me on rough-cast with rocks unthrift
some cryed *Away* my restless eye all the eare lay hush
a bank of flowers nailed a virgin-soile a monstrous
mountaind thing flung clouds ill-shaped eclipsed reply
care's copse was frost within where lay my heart
(pray marke) twixt the brackish ray made abode
there robbed of divers stones my infant buds
so sighd I azure still and listening sought abashed
(though twas mid-day) dispatched an eye asleep
least motion of gladsome lake stormd thus
can both the way and end alas? high spring mere stage
and show broad-eyed the hour a garland wore

Short Fiction

The pages were so laden with description that I grew fitful,
dreaming of a sadness that made the clouds sink, roofs caving under
rain's weight, houses stricken splat in the sea. Thickness pressing
out the color, a white sun very far off. Yet it was a boredom I felt
the story had planned, a light captivity, a cloak with a ribbon
loosely tied at the throat. So I kept returning, room by room, gilded
dust in the slats, hoping one thing would lead to another.
Wondering if the bed would fit me, I laid down under strange
covers, tried not to jostle the sleepers. There I held very still,
waiting to be kissed or heaved awake.

Personification

Mica in cityshadow, a flash across the shoulder. I thought of boxes, a fringe of color, where are you scrawled inside. You could feel it in the distance, a concentration facing you, dark solidity of the hillside across the bay. Lives are stacked in squares. There was a tiny pain then, stab of glass catching sun-glare. It shuts you up. To think of it as a wall, too steep to scale, and someone on the other side shouting.

All the time clearing space, or pressing on each transparency until it became convex, a wavering white line. Like someone's handprint on your skin, a door opens and there you are. But only as you are touched. A spaciousness like a blue net of water, like sleeping late. To find you are not alone there. And who made the darkness plash against your ankles where you had imagined smoothness, a hard enamel.

I thought of a square inside me. Its duration longer than fog or the troubled light on the hill's flank. How running fingers along it is exactly the brightness of holding your breath. Something unrepeatable, a day sliced in half, or a cloud you opened up and slept in. Negative light, all mouths white bone. Mica eyes. To think how long it took, the competence of the ravine inside its tidal edges.

But nowhere discrete, inference of surface like building's shadow.
You never knew you were inside. Your traces unaccountable, called
beloved, graphite on black walls. And no mirror, just the whirr of
voices drawing you close. Come here, a box you drew with your
fingers. How it takes on faint color, breath hot on your shoulder.
Where are you, and then the color dries.

Allegorical

We'd long since misplaced our names, for which
we felt grateful, more concentrated in our resemblances,
able to touch hands through gloves and fog,
and, it seemed, more attuned to scale, our passage
along the icy creek measured against the bleak valley
and the quickness of robins, sundial's weight
in our pockets and swaying sun above. White
clouds assured us the ocean was nearby, perhaps just
beyond the next hill. And so we were disconcerted
by the figures continually marking our progress,
Hopeful, By-Ends, Temporary, and Ignorance, who
spoke to us in familiar tones, guiding us past
treacherous declines and fields of pale, unhappy
flowers. How often they anticipated our
wants—cluster of raisins, loaf of bread.
Their bearing, a certain cast of color in their walk,
was undeniably knowing, uncomfortably so, and we
prayed to be abandoned. Woke once before dusk
and absconded into the foliage, a careless trail of torn ice
and telltale footprints marking our way. But lo,
they loved us despite this injury, and refused to part
with us. And soon our sense of scope had narrowed,
a scrim thrown over the northern sky, these steadfast
figures our only guides. Together we trod a white line
through a forest whose faint light scrambled
our silhouettes. Together along a starlit snow-eyed
shoreline where the frost grazed the sea. Past

canyon-folds whose glowy pages we could not decipher.
The sound of too many footsteps to make count,
erratic breathing all around. If a voice called out
for aid, who held up the lantern for reply?

Partly Cloudy Sedative

A sadness down the throat like a gelcap. Cool plush spread to outer horizon.

The interlocutor: so greedy again, you filled it with, October shaded your eyes, left what remainder.

Assigning a purely decorative meaning. Incessant gauzy hour, god-awful heat, water distracted by minerals.

But it's the silken part. All pale yellow and shivery. Wanton balm soaked in, slow opium vapours.

Brief interval of where did he go? Then that mercury in the stomach again.

: porosity exhausts, pull your skin from, it's leaking all over, the weather while lying down.

Yes, an intrusion. Too much light rain kills the mood.

Hello spotted sunshine. Snagged on ailanthus pith, cat's paw-knotted round the wrist. You ignored my eyes.

: you lost in the grass, lids rimmed with, then geranium mixed on sulfur, embittered in the.

It wasn't like I was looking.

Noon pillows, floats me limnetic. Little twig-petals as ballasts.

: lesions, clocks unspun, black spots in languor, you forgot to.

Lattice-work light says forget it. Collapses in the center, bits of scaffold sprinkling the street.

Here, moth of peace. Lives in pink cloud-striations, sometimes flutters down to secret sheets.

Powdery membrane, pressed by half. Eyes shadowed now.

: where rain collected, feeling is plagiarized, feral scratching means, dug open a.

Whole sky cut out. Glued on white cardboard, tucked in. Day quicksands down, blue-black bedspread.

Like tea poured into a cup.

: trying to tell you, membrane cinching together, sleep frays the first, you left this.

Gemmy sedative dissolve. Steeped gorgeous through marrow, crowflowers.

Metal lockbox in the belly, closes so gently. The shut-in air fondling itself.

: pitching off into, stop tugging at, your mouth caught in the honey, barefaced on.

Wing replicates throat. Fair paper marred. Outside all saline gush, disclaimers blinked out.

: underneath you, drained off, please find your, please find your.

Day ends with streaks. Corolla of fog finds me. A kind of unspining. Then vegetal dark: a ruse I fall for.

A Little Foresight

Something we were saving. Heat sucked into the dirt, one seed sewn into a pocket. For months hot light on the hillside, white mirrors in our eyes. It kept speaking even when we turned away.

Mostly we just waited. Whatever you were holding said goodbye. Dragged along the asphalt, then dropped. The air tried to be patient with us. The snapdragons had a soft fire at their center.

But brown around the edges. We wanted to bless them below suffering, before question. The sun said no. And did we smile then, clasp the seeds in our hands.

Hard to remember where the unspoken was. Inside our mouths, a sunlight we hated. Kept pushing the air, but it would not change. Just stuck us in its bland gummy envelope.

The flower with mirrors in its eye. You said it was never not broken. You said to suffer it. We ran our teeth along the hacked light. Strewn around us like no.

When it was in our hands again, it wasn't what we thought. The sun tore out of our bodies. You said to remember what we couldn't say. How it concerned patience.

Circular

/ sky asleep behind sky / storefronts just resting now / day with rust in its eye / amber and green glass sorted in piles / rot-soured ceiling-boards / sky flees from sky / circular on salvation lodged in the door / waterlogged heap of old news / the dog's old dream / dirt trapped in the eye / green rain rusted in pools / each red a stranger sky / daynotes flood the bed / sky circulates in shallow breaths / knotted cord of rain / the ceiling's torn nest / birds fester and flood the eye / birds dart in then out of smashed storefronts / green rings where water took root / old salvation in a heap on the bed / she's asleep or just resting now / trapdoor sky / shallow scar of sky / ceiling scored in waterlogged amber / gutters salved with rain / livid knot of cars / water pools in rotten wood / birds loose a ringing cry / glass traps one square of day / fleeting tear of sky / rust of eye where green took root / square sky / gutteral sky / red dogs won't rust or rise / sky heaped on the bed / salvation dark / floods the day with sleep / each stranger drives a red car / red knot / trapped sleep / shallow root / greenwater / raineye / floodrot / dirtheap / birdsleep / sky /

Pastoral

the plastic silkier than guilt
         in these brave forests   foursquare & not

     to flee into pines without a racket
of ill-despised items   detached from
       circuit of trade winds

    how I was holding   the little toy whistle

      red teethmarks at the edge
        of debt
sugared berries in capsule

                  packets   &
wanting
    pop-top scrub jay breamgrass rustle
     of texting in trash thicket

        fourscore & unfinished
     construction
         white marriage of
      debris unhallowed   hollow

underfoot sediment cement needles
     cones of some trees mildly
    devoted to their own decay

I was holding & wanting

                    left the inedible wrapping
unconsumed if winged with

                                    loosestrife
                                        nalgene water

                  streaming in reverent fields of
gravel or graves lined with rubber tires

                            more than a tributary
        a tribute to new leaves lapsed

wanting an echo of
        truer invention to ring
the mistrusting surface

      a besmirched seam
                      where oily rain outspent
my fingers
      a small tract   of ready-made earth

           listens for
       the gate-latch

Short Fiction

I slept with a suitcase beside the bed, its emptiness a delay between
pages. I did not dream, and my not-dreaming was the square
gouge of the bag, an exact hole of empty, black hours. When I
woke, the kettle had been calling a long time. Everything waited,
even the snow. Someone knocked at my door, spoke gently to me,
then went away. There were stacks of clothes I had laid out, a brush
matted with hair, the razor with its carnation stains. I piled them
all on the bed, and folded myself up, joint by joint, into the mouth
of the suitcase. It took me in, face-down, and I pulled shut the flap
of light.

The Pilgrim's Progress

thought a ladder leading
                    toward a blue seam unfastened

          thought a lake balancing snowfall

                    thought the gaps in dense foliage
a hand reaching but not found

                              thought glass stood for glass
          something to pour into

as if belong meant the sea and its many
          blazing skins
                    all it set down softly at the feet

                              a mess of wheat for supper

          should never be satisfied with bread
                    after such bounty

and so I slept quietly whole nights together

                    swarms of patched birds
                              & boat-horns plaintively bleating

          never made me restless or desiring

          though the lapping salt-water
                    was almost enough to wake me
          the water a mirror

                  into which I fell headlong
    white-tailed rapids clutching too tight

        so that I was redrawn as a pool
    with the center erased
          or a knot deftly loosened

a horizon smeared with sun

                wading in the black
        the water ran out of my eyes

these were strangers to me

        only a little swill for the body
           up to the knees in mud and water

you could look upon the sun
    as the wine of astonishment

        I was ready sometimes to wish for it

Conjecture

All form returns to form as the body
returns to its hunger as the field
painting wrests apart every color

        or so the day promised, luring
        everything into its arms: and
        demanding of me the same

pooled solid as the eye's iris
sees only discrete planes the way
each breath is a flat table bare
containing itself as a trembling

        promise: flattering to
        think I too was sheltered
        in an ever-expanding circle

at the edge arcs into a gust
coaxing birds in shot-angles black
as the gone cascade alight

        as everyday tasks stacked up:
        sweep, dust, rotate, cough,
        mix, mend, mind, lower

in the field's corner bears a percussive
thrum fusing pain and its echo

          and return: envoy
          to my own renovations:
          the enduring pattern found me

broken as a white plain gives over
to unrest as the sleepless body
returns to its leaden turning
as the forsaken body bends to its shadow

          a bound stranger:
          mistress to a windowed room
          a cry a bed a bending

its reflection shorn as the mother
is a pool a mirror on a darkened lake

Novel Theory

Dissatisfaction pins us transfixed and bound in coherence. This makes a fit subject for fiction, though the icicles will outlast us. The ravine when the wind circulates the day is a novel frame. Possessed by this thought, we wish ourselves a "clear being," but are too full of precipitous action, unaccountable aches in the head, neck, and breast. Farther along, a boy flapping his arms. Should we wave?

The book says bliss disarms itself because one cannot stop watching. We want to be left alone, but the water rumbles along, heedless.

The Journey Conceived As

a way of being held,
the ice covering us over, sun
thinly. Cold sleeves, cold
wind. A split in the river we
said yes to, forgetting
flash-fast with no ground
underneath. Secret orchards
of fish bobbing in nets, a sleek
silt density, water stopping
the ears. Darklit room
greenly swaying, nodded down
in the reeds. Hush now,
you could rest here
in the afterlife of buildings
where everything turns
its back. Time was nailed
to the surface, its eye
glazed over. So we tumbled
gray into error, its
sweet current cradling us
fast. But what net ringed
us wider, the perfect thought
we slept frozen inside
yet could not see? A flicker
of color just beyond
the little wicket-gate—

The Path, Alight

Flag catapulted over

        sea-hedge, four winds
                bodied forth—good afternoon to you—

        red-winged blackbirds unearth a center
anywhere, torn-up air—

        one path split three ways
                straining toward
        scattered
          or surrounded by—

        heel-ball-toe, a figment
          of rhythm that lifts, shudders—

—might as well be snowing—

        an angry murmur in the cedars
and out by the far breakers

                orange dog winding figure-eights—

        waiting for occupation or waiting
          for a different phrasing, a wall
                to stanch the sea—

Down the ladder we went,
            all the way to the far edge—

        swept
as in hand over mouth or feather
        or curtain drawn—

shoreline's unconcealed mystery
        the mind keeps laboring—

—shut your face—
        as we appeared round the bend

                    a barbed message and a bleed
            of yellow, black at belly—

her eyes averted in shame or—

rustle in the sedge-grass
            invisible as the argument
        or lament lingering—

Over and over and over
       spun

   as shouts wrack the birdy air—

        some kind of migrating warbler
   but too mossy in the undergrowth—

     —wait here—
      no

—wait for me—

   listening eyes steady on the side
     of her face—

     rhythm suspended in green

   then poured across
the scratched-out muddy hole—

Farther off
                circle of wet
                        a troubled reflection—

apple rings swarmed by seagulls—

                wind in the teeth
        to interpret silence as—

        —a wan smile—

An arm twisted behind

                              as if to say
              you were mine
                        before you were grass—

                                        wave-furrows the hour

                  a tributary
                              sudden-swift and black—

              what isn't betraying us
                        little by little

shrugs back to dirt at trail's bank—

Returning only to leave anew—

the given path
we could no longer fathom

for it was rotten—

amidst all that brightness

this secret dispersal—

To walk away
          empty-handed—

                    sun-crease in the clearing
          where no thought insists—

          unlonely
                    eyes tracking us all the way

and everything left to itself—

          salt-hollowed log
     three shadows branch sand rills—

                         a sail way down in the sky—

what's unheld forgives

Some Other Time

Turned out of finding into flown, the source only dream-shape, a
color we missed. Suddenly it's day. A gentleness in the grass,
oleander, mimosa, how long have we slept here. So many hours
under eucalyptus canopy, wrack and dazzle of longing we followed
down, peeling back each layer toward what marriage. Such a thing as
the sun, ungovernable, sights the source ever farther, spattered in
diamonds across leaves, runoff, gunmetal planks. And we thinking
we were awake, really only singing, swung. Now the day painted
green, halo of rust at the edge. Look up, you said, the directions
torn, wind stringing white scraps across the brown river, even now
still airborne.

Elsewhere, Thread

was partition, then sidelong—
darling in the mend of brightness

light wrote liar on the eye
ornamental sun limned uncold

so you found scald in the line
called order or ceiling on fire

was almost-true, then midday
cloud broke us into blue muteness

a slight bruise coming awake
papery hand fraying in mine

flush with astound, cut-shadow
eyelid inland a sea of sky

was snowed-in, now unblinded—
pilgrim in the slash of morning

Epistolary

Yes still cold, cyclones

     & spring floods on the radio, not pregnant

no I missed the lunar eclipse
     January drifted in & out

     froze the raised beds

       election season colors its borders

dreamt of you twice
     in the language of childhood

        the newspaper says sorrow
     today the sun slightly

        stray neighbors in civic abeyance

and now crocuses
     the maple's shadow falls across

        not to mention the mice
         in the cupboards

     disliked the rhetoric, "immortal and free"

desired a stricter realism

        the dream
     many hours long
& March is the kids in the park

A Sentimental Journey

Sunrise through vapor, a horizon composed emotionally, the morning passing through us, and here a numberless gaze might pause makeshift in blue aisles, a flock of white sails flashing a reversal into yesterday's harnessed fidelities, homesick passages like midwinter sun slashing ice

The light becoming more itself, even as it withdraws, slipping into sails of a lace dress drying on a line, a sheaf of papers untethered from a desk where you wrote: How terrible we became in the morning before words, how quiet the spring trees were to our one open eye

But waves pull us back, sunburnt country striped with green canopies, near shore the seaweed gathers in rose-shapes, squinting makes the surface thicker, an untrue thought crowning: the you an empty frame the I sleeps inside

What statement of fact unbends with careful handling, pier circumscribed by glass or sunlight distilled in the things it touches, a net with scribbles of fish, pastoral blue that grows softer with prolonged intent, the error we pointed toward became true in the revising

Wind congregates in the right corner, a tract of ultramarine, unenclosed, but for a square of red we move towards, it is traveling into a flag signifying childlike joy, then a postage stamp bearing an old story away

Notes

"Recitative" uses a line, "O but we dreamed to mend," from Yeats's "Nineteen Hundred and Nineteen."

"The New World": this poem owes some of its phrasing to Hobbes's *Leviathan* and a State Farm pamphlet.

"Captivity Narrative" and "The Pilgrim's Progress" incorporate language and narrative framing from Mary Rowlandson's narrative of captivity by the Narragansett and Nashaway Amerindians, *The Sovereignty and Goodness of God: Being a Narrative of the Captivity and Restoration of Mrs. Mary Rowlandson.*

"Character Study": the phrase "no simile runs on all four legs" is by Coleridge, *On the Constitution of the Church and State.*

"The Storm in Fancy's Meadow" is entirely composed of language from George Herbert's "The Pilgrimage" and Henry Vaughn's "Regeneration."

The allegorical names "Hopeful," "By-Ends," "Temporary," and "Ignorance" in "Allegorical" are borrowed from Bunyan's *The Pilgrim's Progress.*

"Conjecture": the lines "each breath is a flat table bare / containing itself as a trembling" were inspired by Victor Grippo's conceptual art piece, *Tables of Work and Reflection* (1978-94), exhibited at the Tate Modern, Britain.

"The Journey Conceived As" draws its closing image of the "little wicket-gate" from Bunyan's *The Pilgrim's Progress.*

"The Path, Alight": this poem was inspired by the central argument of Anne-Lise François's *Open Secrets: The Literature of Uncounted Experience* (Stanford, 2008).